Anne Creatte

POCKET, ROCKET!

Do you have a moment to review this book? Scan this QR code and write a few words from yourself.
I would be very, very grateful.

Anne

GOOD ADVICE

Stand at the doorway and take a picture of the room. This way, you will immediately notice what needs to be changed in the apartment. Walking through the room every day, we no longer see certain things. Try this task, change your perspective.

GOOD ADVICE

Bored with framed pictures? Go to a hardware store and ask for leftover wallpaper. Beautiful wallpaper can be a wonderful and original decoration for your frames in the living room or hallway. Want to save even more? Ask your friends if they have any leftover wallpaper after their renovation, maybe they have something interesting?

____

____

____

GOOD ADVICE

Think about what you notice when you visit someone's home. Is it a gallery of pictures in the bathroom, a beautiful étagère, or maybe an unusual doormat? It's these kinds of elements that make a home unique. What do you think your guests notice when they visit you?

____

____

____

Place a mirror opposite a window to reflect light and make the room feel brighter.
Bonus: Don't be afraid to use unexpected items as decor. This could include things like vintage suitcases, old books, or even musical instruments. For example, you could use a vintage suitcase as a coffee table or a stack of old books to create a unique bookshelf.

NOTE

NOTE